"I Owe You, MOM!" COUPON BOOK

52 Little Ways to Show I Love You Big-time

LENORE SKENAZY & CAROL BOSWELL

A FIRESIDE BOOK
PUBLISHED BY SIMON & SCHUSTER
New York London Toronto Sydney

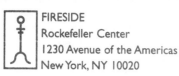
FIRESIDE
Rockefeller Center
1230 Avenue of the Americas
New York, NY 10020

Copyright © 2006 by Lenore Skenazy and Carol Boswell

All rights reserved, including the right of reproduction in whole or in part in any form.
Fireside and colophon are registered trademarks of Simon & Schuster, Inc.

For information regarding special discounts for bulk purchases, please contact Simon & Schuster
Special Sales at 1-800-456-6798 or business@simonandschuster.com.

DESIGN & ILLUSTRATION BY JILL WEBER

Manufactured in the United States of America

10 9 8 7 6 5 4 3 2 1

ISBN-13: 0-978-0-7432-8188-1
ISBN-10:   0-7432-8188-8

Introduction

Dear Mom,

Most kids—even old ones—find it hard to articulate just how much their mothers mean to them. But me . . . I'm worse. There's no way I'll ever be able to tell you how incredibly important you are to me, how encouraging you've been, how much I (despite some immature eye rolling now and then) truly respect you.

So I went and bought this book. There are a lot of things I would like to do—things I haven't done nearly enough, like treat you to tacos, show you how to use your digital camera, borrow some money. . . .

Oh, wait! That's not in here. Anyway, what I really mean is simply this:

Mom, I love you. I owe you. And I want to show you how much. So tear out a coupon and let's get started!

1. A DAY WITHOUT CELL PHONES

Without *my* cell phone,
that is, but *with* you!
Uninterrupted! Undistracted!
Uninfuriating!
Promise!

COUPON

Mom, I owe you!

You may redeem this coupon at any time.

Presented on _____,

with love from _____.

Thanks, Mom!

2. MAKEOVER MADNESS

You or your *car*. Your choice, my treat. I promise you:

- [ ] A shampoo or car wash

- [ ] Highlights or lube job

- [ ] Leg wax or Turtle Wax

Mom, I owe you!

You may redeem this coupon at any time.

Presented on _____,

with love from _____.

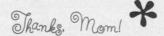

Thanks, Mom! ✳

3. A LESSON IN CYBERSPACE!

I promise to:

❖ IM every week ❖ Teach you how to IM back ❖ Tell you what an IM is
❖ Help you turn on your computer ❖ Okay, help you *buy* a computer

If all this is too much, no worries. I promise to call you once a
week instead. Love ya!

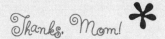

COUPON

Mom, I owe you!

You may redeem this coupon at any time.

Presented on _____,

with love from _____.

Thanks, Mom! ✱

4. IT'S NEVER TOO LATE TO SAY THANK YOU

(Except to Grandma, who's dead)

Dear Mom,

I'll do it. I'm finally ready. I even have the stationery. So here goes:

I promise to write a thank-you note to every relative who ever gave me a gift since I was five.

P.S. Thanks for the stationery

COUPON

Mom, I owe you!

You may redeem this coupon at any time.

Presented on _____,

with love from _____.

Thanks, Mom! ✻

5. I PROMISE THE BEARER OF THIS COUPON

may remove any or all of the following:

- ☐ One objectionable outfit
- ☐ Two novelty T-shirts
- ☐ The entire contents of my laundry bag
  and sell it/them on eBay.

Mom, I owe you!

You may redeem this coupon at any time.

Presented on _____,

with love from _____.

Thanks, Mom!

6. 12:00 12:00 12:00

The witching hour no more! Mom,
I promise to come set your VCR,
DVD player, clock radio, and
whatever else is flashing the
wrong time.

Mom, I owe you!

You may redeem this coupon at any time.

Presented on _____,

with love from _____.

7. HOW CUTE WAS I?

I promise to sit through the whole beautiful story of my birth or adoption.

Mom, I owe you!

You may redeem this coupon at any time.

Presented on _____,

with love from _____.

Thanks, Mom!

8. TRADITION

I promise to revive the family tradition of your choice that died out somewhere along the line. So long as it doesn't involve my singing in front of the relatives.

COUPON

Mom, I owe you!

You may redeem this coupon at any time.

Presented on _____,

with love from _____.

Thanks, Mom!

9. I promise to wear a sweater whenever you're cold.

Mom, I owe you!

You may redeem this coupon at any time.

Presented on _____,

with love from _____.

Thanks, Mom!

10. PHOTO ALBUM ALBATROSS

The album sits empty. The shoe box sits full. Mom, I promise to sort through the pictures and organize them by special occasion: birthdays, vacations, and—where appropriate—divorces. Here's looking at you (in more or less chrono-logical order)!

Mom, I owe you!

You may redeem this coupon at any time.

Presented on _____,

with love from _____.

Thanks, Mom!

11. IMPORTANT!

For as long as I am living at home—or even visiting—I promise I will *not* forget to write down your phone messages. *And* I will leave them where you can find them!

Mom, I owe you!

You may redeem this coupon at any time.

Presented on _____,

with love from _____.

Thanks, Mom! ✲

12. FOR GOODNESS SAKE

I promise to do something good in the world—cook at a soup kitchen, visit the elderly, mentor a kid—something nice like that. Why? Because otherwise I'm going to hell.

Mom, I owe you!

You may redeem this coupon at any time.

Presented on _____,

with love from _____.

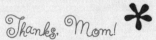

13. THOSE LITTLE WHITE LIES

Remember when I told you nothing much happened at the prom? I promise to finally tell you the truth about that night. Or—come to think of it—maybe the truth about something else. Like the time I said I used my birthday money to buy Grandma some hankies. This coupon is good for the scoop on ONE LIE.

Mom, I owe you!

You may redeem this coupon at any time.

Presented on _____,

with love from _____.

14. YOU'VE GOT TO KNOW WHEN TO HOLD 'EM AND KNOW WHEN TO FOLD 'EM

I promise to teach you the difference and then—it's poker night! I'll take you to a game or bring the game to you! (I need the cash.)

Mom, I owe you!

You may redeem this coupon at any time.

Presented on _____,

with love from _____.

Thanks, Mom!

COUPON

15. SOAP OPERA DIGESTION

For one whole month I promise to watch your favorite soap, figure out who's sleeping with who, *and* talk to you about the characters as if they mattered.

Mom, I owe you!

You may redeem this coupon at any time.

Presented on _____,

with love from _____.

Thanks, Mom!

Vámanos, Mom! I'm taking you out for tacos. My treat!
Come hungry—you're worth the splurge!

Mom, I owe you!

You may redeem this coupon at any time.

Presented on _____,

with love from _____.

Thanks, Mom!

17. YOU GOT IT FOR WHAT?

I promise to act like it's the first time I heard
about the amazing bargain you got on your:

- ☐ Blouse
- ☐ Vacation
- ☐ Meal
- ☐ Husband

Mom, I owe you!

You may redeem this coupon at any time.

Presented on _____,

with love from _____.

Thanks, Mom!

18. A DAY OF OPRAH-FICATION

Together we will:

Read her magazine 📖 Watch her show 📺 Discuss her current book selection. Cook light 🍲 Feel conflicting emotions about Dr. Phil. Get in touch with our inner light 🕯 Figure out what that inner light *is*. Replace inner light if it has burned out 💡 Change our hairstyles 💇 Change our lifestyles. Make peace with our inner demons. Feed demons a nice piece of marble cheesecake, if need be.

Go on a diet Go off a diet

Mom, I owe you!

You may redeem this coupon at any time.

Presented on _____,

with love from _____.

Thanks, Mom!

19. CAMP LETTER DAY!

You saved those letters for someday. That some-day is *today*! So get them out and I promise we'll read them together!

But not in a tent.

Mom, I owe you!

You may redeem this coupon at any time.

Presented on _____,

with love from _____.

Thanks, Mom!

20.

I promise to go back to my original gender,
or at least fake it, at your funeral.

Mom, I owe you!

You may redeem this coupon at any time.

Presented on _____,

with love from _____.

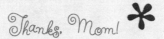

Thanks, Mom!

21. WALLET PHOTO UPDATE

Out with the old, in with the new. I promise to give you a current wallet-sized photo of me, but I can't promise that it will be as cute as the one of me without my front teeth. Nothing ever will be.

Mom, I owe you!

You may redeem this coupon at any time.

Presented on _____,

with love from _____.

Thanks, Mom!

22.

I promise to take on all your calories for one day! I haven't quite worked out the physics of this, but I swear—the calories are going to go to my hips.

COUPON

Mom, I owe you!

You may redeem this coupon at any time.

Presented on _____,

with love from _____.

23. SMILE, MOM!

You can even say cheese! because I promise to show you how to use your digital camera and download the photos to your computer. By the end of the day, we *will* have a print! (I hope.)

Mom, I owe you!

You may redeem this coupon at any time.

Presented on _____,

with love from _____.

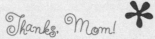

24. DIVA FOR A DAY

You deserve it (certainly more than Star Jones)! I promise to be your personal assistant for a day. Snap your fingers and I am at your command. Choose five demeaning tasks from the list below and I will:

☐ Wash the dog ☐ Perfume the dog ☐ Find your reading glasses (maximum 10 times) ☐ Answer your phone in a French or British accent ☐ Hold your umbrella (even if it's sunny) ☐ Buy you a bauble at some ridiculously expensive boutique ☐ Return it the same day ☐ Complain to 10 people for you ☐ Ask for your autograph

Mom, I owe you!

You may redeem this coupon at any time.

Presented on _____,

with love from _____.

Thanks, Mom!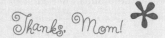

25. IPOD, YOURPOD

Tell me your favorite songs of all time, and I promise I will download them to an iPod and show you how to use it. Plug in and rock out, Mom!

Mom, I owe you!

You may redeem this coupon at any time.

Presented on _____,

with love from _____.

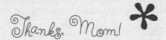

Thanks, Mom!

26. EXTREME BONDING

Let's go get matching tattoos, Mom. No butt butterflies, I promise. (Butt skulls? Another story.)

Mom, I owe you!

You may redeem this coupon at any time.

Presented on _____,

with love from _____.

Thanks, Mom!

27. ONE DAY OF HOUSECLEANING

That's what I'm promising you!
Your place or mine—I'll make it shine.

COUPON

Mom, I owe you!

You may redeem this coupon at any time.

Presented on _____,

with love from _____.

Thanks, Mom! ✻

28. MEDICAL DAY

Choose any or all of the following, Mom, because I promise to:

✚ Listen to you tell me about your ailments ✚ Look up your symptoms ✚ Find out if they're catching ✚ Go with you to the doctor ✚ Ask all the questions you're too embarrassed to ask ✚ Fetch your prescription ✚ Fetch your slippers ✚ Sympathize, empathize, and eat chocolate with you (unless it really *is* diabetes)

Mom, I owe you!

You may redeem this coupon at any time.

Presented on _____,

with love from _____.

Thanks, Mom!

29. WHAT YOU LIKE, I LIKE (OR AT LEAST I'LL GIVE IT A SHOT)

That very special movie
Or show that's on TV,
That ten-part Yanni thingy
Or ethnic songs CD.
Whatever it is that moves you,
Whatever you want to share,
I'll watch or listen with you
And not slump in my chair.
We'll weep or laugh together,

We'll sigh and maybe nod,
And when the thing is over
I will not shout, "Thank God!"

I promise to enjoy—yes,
enjoy—one TV, movie or
audio experience with you.
My treat!

Mom, I owe you!

You may redeem this coupon at any time.

Presented on _____,

with love from _____.

Thanks, Mom!

30. OOPS

Mom, I promise not to do whatever I did
last week that really annoyed you.
And I apologize, too.

Mom, I owe you!

You may redeem this coupon at any time.

Presented on _____,

with love from _____.

Thanks, Mom!

31. SHOW AND TELL

I promise I will *show* up wherever your friends congregate and you can *tell* them everything about me, right down to my shoe size and SAT scores, with every intention of making them wish they had a kid like me.

Mom, I owe you!

You may redeem this coupon at any time.

Presented on _____,

with love from _____.

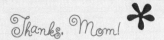

Thanks, Mom! ✱

32. YOUR PERSONAL CFO

Get out the paperwork and shove it at me, Mom.
Taxes, insurance forms, parking ticket pleas—I promise
I'll fill them out, file, or mail them—whatever
needs to be done.
I'll even bring stamps.

COUPON

Mom, I owe you!

You may redeem this coupon at any time.

Presented on _____,

with love from _____.

Thanks, Mom!

33.

Emeril. Bam! That's me, the evening of your choice.
I'll use everything I've learned from the Food Channel
to prepare you an *extraordinary* meal.

P.S. What's a shallot?

Mom, I owe you!

You may redeem this coupon at any time.

Presented on _____,

with love from _____.

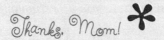

Thanks, Mom!

34.

Dear Mom,

I promise to honor your living will.
And I promise to write one, too.
Now—back to cheerier coupons.

Mom, I owe you!

You may redeem this coupon at any time.

Presented on _____,

with love from _____.

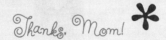

Thanks, Mom! *

35. ATTIC AND/OR BASEMENT DAY

I promise we'll spend the day of your choice
weeping sweet tears over tiny garments and
other old clothes that smell funky.

And then we'll call Goodwill.

Mom, I owe you!

You may redeem this coupon at any time.

Presented on _____,

with love from _____.

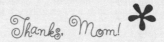

36. YOU-WERE-RIGHT, I-WAS-WRONG DAY

And here it is, in writing.
It's never too late to admit you were
absolutely right about everything.

And I promise to listen better
for the next twenty-four hours.

Mom, I owe you!

You may redeem this coupon at any time.

Presented on _____,

with love from _____.

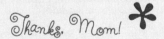

Thanks, Mom! ✳

37. SHAPE UP!

Set the alarm. Get out the sweats. Because I promise to be your personal trainer for a week! Now drop and give me fifty.

Mom, I owe you!

You may redeem this coupon at any time.

Presented on _____,

with love from _____.

Thanks, Mom! ✳

38. I CAN TAKE IT!

Go ahead and tell that embarrassing story about
me to a friend of mine of the opposite sex.

I promise not to hold it against you forever.

COUPON

Mom, I owe you!

You may redeem this coupon at any time.

Presented on _____,

with love from _____.

Thanks. Mom! *

39. A DAY WITHOUT GIMMIES

I promise I will absolutely *not* ask you *all day* to

- ✤ Buy me something
- ✤ Mail me something
- ✤ Lend me money (unless you really
  don't need that $20)

Mom, I owe you!

You may redeem this coupon at any time.

Presented on _____,

with love from _____.

Thanks, Mom! ✱

40. GET OUT THE CABBAGE

I know that someday I will regret not knowing how to make the secret family recipe, so I'm waiting for you in the kitchen. Teach it to me. I promise I'll pass it on to the next generation.

COUPON

Mom, I owe you!

You may redeem this coupon at any time.

Presented on _____,

with love from _____.

Thanks, Mom!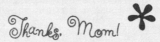

41. I'M YOU!

Send me in your place to visit a relative, run an errand, or simply make an appearance at a place you don't want to go. You're off the hook! I promise to represent you well.

Mom, I owe you!

You may redeem this coupon at any time.

Presented on _____,

with love from _____.

Thanks, Mom! ✳

42. MAKE ME A MATCH

I promise that I will not object if you submit 1 (one) photo of me along with a loving if inaccurate description of me to an online dating service.

Mom, I owe you!

You may redeem this coupon at any time.

Presented on _____,

with love from _____.

Thanks, Mom!

43. NO PICTURES, PLEASE

Dorky, perhaps. Nonetheless I promise to wear *in public* for *an entire day* one item of clothing that you gave me.

Mom, I owe you!

You may redeem this coupon at any time.

Presented on _____,

with love from _____.

Thanks, Mom!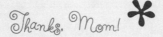

44. I PROMISE TO VISIT A LOVED ONE'S

☐ Home

☐ Hospital room

☐ Assisted living facility

☐ Locked ward

on a nice weekend day. And no sour face, either.

Mom, I owe you!

You may redeem this coupon at any time.

Presented on _____,

with love from _____.

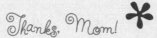

Thanks, Mom! ✻

45. A HOLE IN ONE

That's what I promise to have in some part
of my body when I take out the ear, nose,
or belly-button ring that you think is gross.

Mom, I owe you!

You may redeem this coupon at any time.

Presented on _____,

with love from _____.

Thanks, Mom! ✳

46. ROSES ARE RED

Violets are blue.
So why don't I ever
Send any to you?

Mom, I will! Next time you need a little cheering up,
just give me a call. Say the secret word, "pollinate,"
and I promise to send or come by with flowers for
you.

Mom, I owe you!

You may redeem this coupon at any time.

Presented on _____,

with love from _____.

Thanks, Mom!

COUPON

47. SALSA, SINGING, OR SPANISH?

Sign us up for a semester of one of 'em.
I just hope it's not salsa or singing.

Mom, I owe you!

You may redeem this coupon at any time.

Presented on _____,

with love from _____.

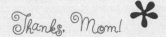

Thanks, Mom! ✱

48. FLUFFY—THIS TIME I *MEAN* IT.

Mom, I know I never took care of Fluffy when I was growing up, but this time, I *will*. I promise to take care of all your pet's needs the next time you are away.

Unless the new Fluffy is a Rottweiler.

Mom, I owe you!

You may redeem this coupon at any time.

Presented on _____,

with love from _____.

Thanks, Mom!

49. I'M MOVING OUT—OR IN

Your choice. I promise I will do either
one of these for you for a week.

COUPON

Mom, I owe you!

You may redeem this coupon at any time.

Presented on _____,

with love from _____.

Thanks, Mom! ✳

50. WHATEVER HAPPENED TO WHAT'S HIS NAME?

I promise to help you track down your first sweetheart, your friend who moved away, or even that jerk who still owes you money.

COUPON

Mom, I owe you!

You may redeem this coupon at any time.

Presented on _____,

with love from _____.

Thanks. Mom! ✳

51. MATURITY AT LAST

Dear Mom,

I know you're not just my mom but a human being. I promise to try to appreciate you as one.

Let's see how long this lasts.

COUPON

Mom, I owe you!

You may redeem this coupon at any time.

Presented on _____,

with love from _____.

Thanks, Mom!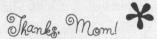

52. I PROMISE I WILL NEVER HAVE SEX WITHOUT A CONDOM!

Mom, I owe you!

You may redeem this coupon at any time.

Presented on _____,

with love from _____.

Thanks, Mom! ✳